ROCKS AND MINERALS

SOIL

by Rebecca E. Hirsch

Content Consultant
Daniel Richter Jr.
Professor of Soils and Ecology
Duke University

Core Library

An Imprint of Abdo Publishing
www.abdopublishing.com

www.abdopublishing.com

Published by Abdo Publishing, a division of ABDO, PO Box 398166, Minneapolis, Minnesota 55439. Copyright © 2015 by Abdo Consulting Group, Inc. International copyrights reserved in all countries. No part of this book may be reproduced in any form without written permission from the publisher. Core Library™ is a trademark and logo of Abdo Publishing.

Printed in the United States of America, North Mankato, Minnesota
042014
092014

THIS BOOK CONTAINS
RECYCLED MATERIALS

Cover Photo: iStockphoto/Thinkstock
Interior Photos: iStockphoto/Thinkstock, 1, 8, 30, 37, 45; Keith Levit/Thinkstock, 4; Eyecandy Images/Thinkstock, 7; Red Line Editorial, 10; Ken Schulze/Shutterstock Images, 12; Shutterstock Images, 14, 18, 27, 35, 42 (top), 42 (bottom); Galyna Andrushko/Shutterstock Images, 16; Top Photo Corporation/Thinkstock, 21; Catherine Murray/Shutterstock Images, 24; Sokolov Alexey/Shutterstock Images, 29; Monkey Business Images/Shutterstock Images, 32; Ross D. Franklin/AP Images, 38; Phaitoon Sutunyawatchai/Shutterstock Images, 40; Bogdan Wankowicz/Shutterstock Images, 43

Editor: Lauren Coss
Series Designer: Becky Daum

Library of Congress Control Number: 2014932352

Cataloging-in-Publication Data
Hirsch, E. Rebecca.
 Soil / Rebecca E. Hirsch.
   p. cm. -- (Rocks and minerals)
Includes bibliographical references and index.
ISBN 978-1-62403-391-9
1. Soils--Juvenile literature.   I. Title.
577--dc23
                                    2014932352

CONTENTS

CHAPTER ONE

WHAT IS SOIL?

S oil is all around you. To find a place on land without soil, you would have to climb to an icy or rocky mountaintop. Or you could journey to a newly erupted volcano, where hardened lava covers the ground. You'll find soil under your feet almost anywhere you can walk.

Soil is an important substance. It provides materials for buildings and helps support those

Soil is essential for life on Earth. It helps us grow food and recycle nutrients.

buildings. Soil even holds clues to the past. Archaeologists dig through soil to learn about ancient civilizations. Scientists can even study the soil itself to learn about the past!

But what is soil exactly? You can think of soil as the top layer of Earth's surface. The soil layer can be only one foot (0.3 m) deep. In some places, however, the soil layer is more than 100 feet (30 m) deep.

What's more, the soil layer is alive. It is filled with tiny living beings called microbes. Just one tablespoon (14.8 mL) of soil contains more microbes than there are humans on Earth. Many

The Dirt on Dirt

Scientists use the term "soil," but you might call it "dirt." What's the difference? Dirt is soil found in places where it is not wanted. You track dirt inside the house on your shoes. Dirt finds a home between your toes and under your fingernails. Removing dirt can be difficult because water alone does not wash it away. You need to use soap as well. Particles of soap stick to particles of dirt, allowing water to remove the grime.

The uppermost part of the soil is usually best for growing crops.

microbes have a scientific name, but most don't have a name yet.

All soil contains living beings and the remains of living beings, which together are called organic matter. Soil also contains broken-down bits of rocks. Finally, in the pores between the particles of rock and organic matter, soil contains air and water. Organic matter, crushed rock, air, and water: these four elements are found in all soil.

Soil Texture

Soil is very diverse. It differs greatly from one part of the world to another. It even differs from one side

Red soil can be seen in the savannahs of Kenya, Africa.

of the street to the other. Soil comes in many colors, including brown, black, red, yellow, green, blue, and even white. The brown and black colors usually come from organic matter. Other colors come from minerals in the bits of rock that make up the soil. Minerals are substances formed naturally within the earth that do not come from animals or plants. Red soil has a large amount of the mineral iron. White soils often contain calcium.

Soil has different textures too. It can feel slippery, smooth, or grainy. The sizes of the particles of rock in the soil determine the texture. You can learn a great deal about soil by grabbing a handful and giving it a squeeze.

Soil that falls apart when you squeeze it contains a large amount of sand. Sandy soils have big bits of crushed rock that are large enough that you can see the particles. Soils with a great deal of sand feel gritty. They dry quickly after a rainfall because there are big spaces between the bits of rock. Water runs right through the spaces.

Some soil feels powdery and smooth. These soils contain a large amount of silt. Silt is made of tiny particles of rock. Silty soil is often good for

Quicksand

If you are walking on sandy soil, you'd better be careful. You do not want to get sucked into quicksand! Quicksand is sandy soil filled with water. The soupy mixture cannot support weight, so if you step on it, you sink. The most likely places to find quicksand are riverbanks, lakeshores, marshes, and beaches. If you are stuck in quicksand, don't struggle. You'll sink deeper. Just relax, and your body will float.

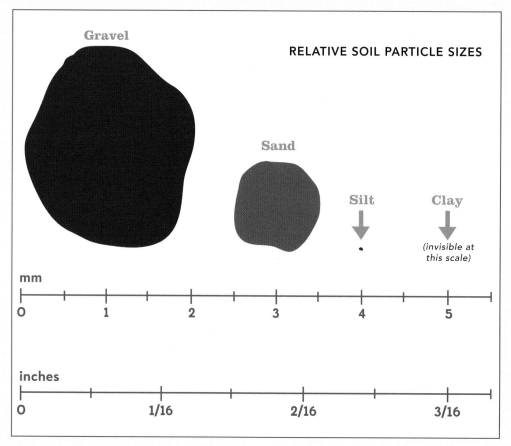

RELATIVE SOIL PARTICLE SIZES

Gravel

Sand

Silt

Clay

(invisible at this scale)

mm

0   1   2   3   4   5

inches

0   1/16   2/16   3/16

Soil Particles

This diagram shows the sizes of soil particles. How does the information in the diagram compare with the details you read in the text? How does seeing the particle sizes help you understand the different kinds of soil?

growing plants, but it is easily blown away by wind or washed away by a flood.

Other soil feels slippery or sticky and forms a ball when you squeeze it. This soil contains a large amount of clay. Clay particles are so small you need a powerful microscope to see them. The spaces between the particles are so tiny that water can't drain through them. Because of this, clay holds water well. People make clay into bowls and jugs.

Finally, there is a kind of soil that feels soft and crumbly and looks dark, almost like chocolate cake. This soil is called loam. It is a mix of sand and silt with a little bit of clay. If you find loam, you might want to grab a shovel and some seeds. This is the best soil for growing plants!

FURTHER EVIDENCE

There is quite a bit of information about soil in Chapter One. What was one of the chapter's main points? What are some pieces of evidence that support this idea? Visit the website at the link below. Does the information on the website support this chapter's main point? Write a few sentences using new information from the website as evidence to support a main point in this chapter.

The Earth's Soil
www.mycorelibrary.com/soil

CHAPTER TWO

ROCK INTO SOIL

Have you ever recycled an object? Nature recycles too. In nature, rocks form, are destroyed, and form again. This recycling process is called the rock cycle.

Rocks form when a volcano erupts. The molten, or liquid, rock cools and hardens, making new rocks. This bare rock is not yet soil. But it can become soil if

Plants wear down rocks when they grow between them. Soil sometimes forms from this type of weathering.

Cracks in rocks are often the result of freezing and thawing water.

it breaks down into small particles. This process takes a long, long time.

When rocks sit at Earth's surface, they break down in several ways. This process is called weathering, and it can take millions of years. Weathering breaks down rocks into smaller particles. As a result, the mineral part of soil forms. The soil contains the same minerals as the original rock.

Sun, wind, rain, ice, and plants cause weathering. Sometimes rain beats down on a rock, dissolving bits of it. The water may trickle into a crack and freeze. As the water freezes, it pushes outward and cracks the rock.

Sometimes plants grow on rocks. The roots seek out cracks in the rock where water and nutrients are stored. As the roots grow, they wedge the rocks apart. This is another example of weathering.

How Soil Forms

Plants grow in the new soil created by weathering. They dig deep roots, creating holes for air and water. They drop dead leaves, needles, and twigs onto the soil. Animals, such as earthworms, ants, and rodents, live in the soil. They mix the organic plant matter into the soil and create tunnels where water and air flow. Microbes help decompose the remains of living things. They add organic matter to the minerals in the soil. The decayed plants and animals become a brown or black material known as humus.

More plants grow in rain forests than deserts because of the deep, rich soil.

Soil may take thousands or even millions of years to form. Soil forms more quickly in warm, moist places. It forms slowly in cold or dry places. This is why a rain forest often has deeper soil than a desert.

As time passes, soil changes. In fact, soil never stays the same. The parts of soil—minerals, water, air, organic matter, and living creatures—are always changing.

Soil Layers

If you've ever dug a deep hole, you may have noticed layers in the earth. As soil forms, it builds up in different layers, known as horizons. Altogether, horizons form the soil.

The top layer is the O horizon. It contains a large number of plants and insects. It also has humus. In some places, the O horizon is very thick. In other places, it might not be present at all.

The next layer is the A horizon. This layer is made mostly of minerals from the original rock, along with some organic matter. Plant roots grow in the A horizon. It also is home to other animals, such as rodents and insects. As rain soaks through the A horizon, it washes away very small particles of clay and some of the minerals. The O and A horizons together are known as topsoil.

Next is the B horizon, also called the subsoil. This layer contains the minerals and clay that have

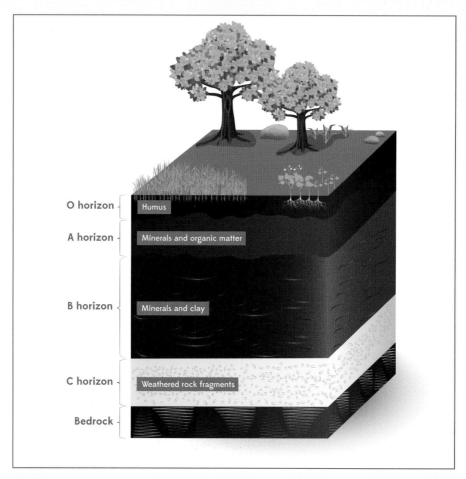

O horizon — Humus

A horizon — Minerals and organic matter

B horizon — Minerals and clay

C horizon — Weathered rock fragments

Bedrock —

Soil Layers

This diagram shows the layers that make up soil. After reading about these layers, what did you imagine they looked like? How have your ideas changed? How does seeing the layers help you better understand soil?

washed downward from the topsoil. It has less organic material than the upper two layers.

The deepest layer of soil is the C horizon. This layer is the original rock that has begun to weather.

The C horizon has very little organic matter. Few plant roots grow deep in the C horizon. Beneath the C horizon lies the bedrock.

Soil around the World

What is the soil like where you live? Soil in one place can be very different from soil in another place. For this reason, scientists put soils into different groups. The groups are based on many factors, including the soil's color, its chemical makeup, and the types of plants and animals living in it. Soil groups are closely tied to the biomes where the soils are found. For example, frozen soils are in a different group than rain forest soils. And all frozen soils are similar to one another, even if they are in different parts of the world.

Frozen soils form on the tops of high mountains or in very cold places. These soils have a large amount of organic matter. The ground is too cold for organic matter to decompose, so it stays trapped in the soil.

The Leaning Tower of Pisa

Why does the Leaning Tower of Pisa lean? It is built on soft soil. The soil in Pisa, Italy, is so soft, many buildings lean. But the famous tower leans at such an extreme angle that officials worried the building might collapse. To save it, workers used a drill to slowly remove soil from one side of the tower. As the soil settled, the workers used cables to pull the tower upright. The work took several years. By 2001 the tower's lean was reduced by 17 inches (43 cm).

Desert soils get very little rainfall. Even though these soils are very dry, they can grow a great deal of food if they have extra water. Because there is so little rain, nutrients in desert soil are not washed away as quickly as in other places.

Prairie soils receive more rainfall than deserts but not as much as forests. Grasses dig their roots deep into the soil. When the grasses decompose, they make prairie soils rich in organic matter.

Forest soils receive a large amount of rain. The water washes the nutrients and clay particles downward, forming a layer of clay. In tropical rain

The tower in Pisa, Italy, still leans, but it was saved thanks to workers' efforts.

Pompeii

Volcanic soil is excellent for growing crops. But living near an active volcano can be risky! Pompeii was an ancient Italian city near the volcano Mount Vesuvius. In 79 CE, Mount Vesuvius erupted. Ash rolled down the mountain and quickly buried the city. Many people did not escape. As years passed, people forgot about Pompeii. Then in 1748, explorers began digging where Pompeii once stood. They were surprised to find that the ash had preserved Pompeii as it was at the moment of the eruption. Today Pompeii is famous as a city frozen in time.

forests, there is so much rain that the nutrients wash away.

New soils form near volcanoes. These soils are made of volcanic ash. They have a large amount of nutrients from deep within the earth. Volcanic soils are good for growing plants.

Finally, there are urban soils, which are found in cities. Humans have changed these soils. They may be polluted with salt from winter roads, oil from cars, and other chemicals. Humans may have also added nutrients to urban soils to make them better for growing plants.

Archaeologists study soil to learn about ancient people. One group of archaeologists studied an ancient Mayan site in Mexico. They found high levels of phosphorus in the soil. They think this means the site was once an open-air market:

> Dr. Terry's team took several hundred samples of soil. . . . Food and other organic matter might decay, but they leave chemical traces that survive in the soil. All food materials contain phosphorus, a particularly durable marker of food from long ago.
>
> The researchers applied a dilute acid to the samples and filtered the resulting solution. Exposed to a light from a portable laboratory, the phosphorus in the soil emitted a blue glow; the bluer it was, the greater the amount of [phosphorus]. Most samples from the site showed phosphorus concentrations 40 times higher than in surrounding soils.

Source: John Noble Wilford. "Ancient Yucatán Soils Point to Maya Market, and Market Economy." New York Times. The New York Times Company, January 8, 2008. Web. Accessed November 11, 2013.

What's the Big Idea?

Take a close look at this excerpt. Why are archaeologists investigating phosphorus in the soil? Pick out two details about how they tested for phosphorus. What can you tell about the ancient site based on this experiment?

ONE HANDFUL OF SOIL

Next time you're outside, scoop up some soil. Your hand is now filled with living creatures. Most are too tiny to see without a microscope. These microbes are small, but each one has a job to do.

You may hold 100 billion single-celled bacteria in your handful of soil. You'll also find millions of fungi. Some fungi are too small to see with just your eyes.

Soil is full of life. One square yard (0.8 sq m) may contain 100 to 500 worms.

Others, such as mushrooms, are bigger. The above-ground part of a mushroom grows from long threads in the soil.

Living Soil

Bacteria and fungi have important jobs to do. Most act as decomposers. When a living being dies and returns to the soil, decomposers break it down. They help recycle dead plants and animals into humus. As the humus breaks down, plants can use its nutrients.

Other soil microbes live together with plants. These bacteria and fungi help plants get the nutrients they need. Some

Termites and Soil

Some termites live in homes built from a mixture of soil, saliva, and termite waste. The mound looks solid from the outside, but inside it is full of holes. The mound has many places for the termite colony to live, including chambers for the king and queen. The mound also has places to store wood, a termite's favorite food. The mound even has gardens, where termites grow fungi. The termites eat the fungi, which helps them get nutrients from the wood they eat.

Termites and other organisms help make the soil richer for growing plants.

take nitrogen from the air and turn it into a nutrient plants can use.

Not all organisms in a handful of soil are microscopic. You might find ants, beetles, termites, spiders, centipedes, or millipedes. Some of these creatures eat plants and animals. Others act as shredders. They chew up bits of dead plants.

You'll find plenty of worms in soil. Some worms are so tiny you can't see them with your eyes alone. Others, such as earthworms, are bigger. Earthworms eat plants and organic matter. They recycle nutrients

All about Earthworms

Have you ever seen a soft, slippery earthworm? One acre (0.4 ha) of soil can be home to 1,000 pounds (450 kg) of earthworms. Earthworms are good at building soil. With their shovel-like mouths, earthworms eat rotting plants and animals. They turn this dead matter into rich fertilizer. Some earthworms are only one inch (2.5 cm) long. Others can grow to three feet (0.9 m)!

and make the soil richer. As they burrow, they mix the soil and create spaces for air and water.

Animals

Some underground creatures are even bigger than insects and worms. Large animals also live under the earth. Moles dig long tunnels underground. They gnaw on plant roots. Using their keen noses, moles sniff out earthworms and insects to eat. All that digging makes a mole strong—and hungry. Moles eat half their weight in food every day.

Badgers use their powerful legs to dig underground burrows that they live in. Badgers eat small rodents that live underground. Like other soil-

Young red foxes live in holes their mothers dig in the soil.

dwelling animals, badgers are specially adapted to life underground. They have an extra set of eyelids to help keep soil out of their eyes.

You'll find many other animals living in the soil. Foxes raise their young in underground dens. Prairie dogs live together in burrows that have many tunnels and chambers. A burrowing owl builds its nest in a hole in the ground. It may dig its own burrow or use

Healthy soils help filter water and air.

one made by other animals, such as prairie dogs, skunks, armadillos, or turtles.

Life-giving Soil

Soil gives life to many plants and animals, including humans! Plants get their minerals and water from soil. Animals get nutrients by eating plants. Farm animals, wild animals, and fish all eat plants. Other animals eat these plant-eating animals. So even carnivores get their nutrients from soil. Next time you go to the supermarket, take a good look around. Much of the food you see can be traced back to soil.

Healthy soils do more than just give us food. Soils recycle nutrients so the nutrients can be used over and over again.

Soil can keep you healthy in other ways too. Microbes in soil are used to make life-saving medicines. Antibiotics from the soil can help your body fight off germs.

EXPLORE ONLINE

Chapter Three discusses the organisms that live in soil. The website below has even more information about creatures that live in soil. As you know, every source is different. How is the information in the website different from the information in this chapter? What information is the same? How do the two sources present information differently?

Soil Field Guide
www.mycorelibrary.com/soil

CHAPTER FOUR

NATURAL EROSION

I f you have ever tracked dirt into your home, you know soil doesn't always stay in one place. Sometimes it travels from the place where it was made to another location. This natural process is called erosion. It is part of the rock cycle.

Soil moves in many ways aside from being carried on your feet. Wind blows across bare earth and lifts loose soil into the air. Rain falls on exposed soil and

Humans are often responsible for transporting soil from place to place.

loosens the soil particles. When rain is heavy, water flows over the surface of the ground. The loose particles wash away.

Once soil washes into a stream or river, it is no longer called soil. It is called sediment. In fast-moving water, sediment stays suspended, making the water muddy. In slow-moving water, sediment settles in layers on the bottom of the body of water.

Plants slow down erosion. They help to keep soil in place. In prairies, grasses dig their roots deep and protect soil from floods and wind. Soil microbes also do their part to prevent erosion. They help soil particles stick together so they don't blow or wash away.

Dirt Detectives

At a crime scene, police can use the dirt to help solve the crime. No two soils are exactly alike. Scientists can take a sample of the dirt and study it in a lab. They may study the soil's color, minerals, and particle size, as well as different combinations of bacteria in the soil. Scientists may even try to match dirt from a suspect's shoes to the dirt found at the scene of the crime.

Tree roots help hold the soil together.

Erosion Problem

Today erosion happens much faster than in the past. More than 26 billion tons (24 billion metric tons) of soil blow or wash away each year. That is ten times faster than soil forms.

In the past, trees, grasses, and other plants covered more of the ground. But people have cut down trees for wood or paper. They have cleared away plants to make room for buildings and roads.

When the soil is bare, each raindrop hits the ground like a tiny rocket. Soil sprays high into the air.

35

Without plant roots to hold down the soil, it is more easily swept away by wind or washed away by water.

Farming also can cause erosion. In spring many farmers till, or turn over, the soil before planting a new crop. The pores between soil particles collapse, and the soil breaks apart. It can then blow or wash away.

Desertification

Sometimes erosion can turn good farmland into desert. This is called desertification. This happened once in the United States. In the 1920s, farmers in the western states plowed the prairie. They planted wheat and other crops where tall prairie grasses once stood.

In the 1930s, a drought struck the western states. Farmers kept plowing and planting, but their crops would not grow because there was not enough water. Without plants, winds blew away the soil in great clouds known as dust storms. Some dust storms lasted for hours. People called them "black blizzards."

The places hardest hit by the dust storms became known as the Dust Bowl. This included parts of

Tilling the land mixes up the natural layers of soil, which causes the soil to erode more easily.

In 2011 a dust storm nearly 100 miles (160 km) wide blew through Phoenix, Arizona.

Kansas, Oklahoma, Texas, Colorado, and New Mexico. The dust storms also blew east. In the eastern states, they created muddy rain and black snow.

After the drought, US farmers learned to use better farming methods. They changed the way they plowed the land. They planted trees between fields to slow the wind.

In the United States, dust storms are not as severe today as they once were, but they can still be a problem. In other parts of the world, such as China, desertification remains a big issue.

Protecting Soil

To keep soil from eroding, many farmers now use better plowing methods. Some farmers plow in curving rows that follow the shape of the land. The rows create trenches to catch water and keep soil from running off the land. Other farmers do not plow their soil at all.

Farmers also know to keep soil covered. The best kind of cover is called a cover crop. It is a living cover of green plants that prevents soil from splashing or blowing

Cover Crops

Cover crops, such as clover, rye, and beans, are a great way to improve soil. They help keep bare soil covered. Later, they can be plowed into the earth to add nutrients. Cover crops also keep the ground cool. Uncovered soil heats up quickly under the hot sun. The hotter the soil gets, the faster water evaporates. Covered soil needs less water. Cover crops provide shade from the sun, keeping the ground cool and moist.

Crop rotation prevents one plant from robbing too many nutrients from the soil.

away. Some cover crops even give nutrients back to the soil.

Farmers protect their soil in many ways. One way is to plant a different crop each year. A farmer might plant corn one year, beans the next year, and alfalfa the year after that. This is called crop rotation.

It is important to keep soil from eroding. Soil is home to many plants and animals. Many creatures rely on soil to help produce their food—including humans! Next time you have a handful of dirt, look at it closely. What is the soil like where you live?

In the 1930s, soil erosion caused giant dust storms across the Great Plains. Clouds of dust swallowed huge areas of land. The region became known as the Dust Bowl. This newspaper article describes one of the dust storms:

> *Another major dust storm, causing confusion and widespread property damage, rolled eastward tonight across the Midwest plains.*
>
> *Traffic was paralyzed by both land and air. Schools were closed. Business was tied up. Street lights were turned on in midday, blinking eerily in the heavy haze.*
>
> *Human lives were threatened by traffic dangers and possible suffocation. Livestock suffered.*

Source: The Associated Press. "Black Dust Storm Chokes Midwest; Land and Air Traffic Halts and Schools Close as Darkness of Night Descends." New York Times. *The New York Times Company*, March 21, 1935. Web. Accessed November 21, 2013.

Back It Up

The author of this article uses evidence to support a point. Write a paragraph describing the author's point. Then write down two or three pieces of evidence the author uses to make the point.

Soil Shake-up

Find a clear glass or plastic jar with a lid. Fill the jar one-third full with soil. Add water almost to the top. Tightly screw on the lid. Shake for 15 to 20 seconds, and then leave the jar in a safe place overnight. Take a look the next day. What do you see? The bottom layer contains sand and rocks. The middle layer is silt. The top layer is clay. Why do you think these layers formed the way they did? Write a journal entry describing your experiment.

How are the layers of soil in your jar similar to the layers you see here?

What's in Your Soil?

Find a place where you can investigate the soil where you live. If there are dead leaves on the ground, examine the undersides of the leaves. Do you see any white threads? Those are fungi. Next dig up some soil. You may find earthworms. You may even find animal tunnels or burrows. You will probably find many plant roots too. Take notes about your findings. When you're done examining the soil, put it back where you found it.

Many living things thrive in decomposing leaves and the soil beneath them.

Beans will sprout quickly in nutrient-rich soil.

The Best Soil

Gather some flowerpots or yogurt containers with holes punched in the bottom. Ask an adult to help you find three different types of soil, such as potting soil, sand, and soil from a flower bed. Next fill each container with a different soil. Label your containers so you know which soil is in each one. Then plant two bean seeds about 0.5 inch (1.3 cm) deep in each container. Keep the soil moist but not soggy. Which beans sprouted first? After a few days, measure the bean plants. Write your measurements in a chart. Which soil do you think is best for growing beans?

Why Do I Care?

Soil is essential for life on Earth. How does soil affect your life? Are there objects or materials that might not exist without it? How might your life be different without soil? Use your imagination!

Take a Stand

Chapter Four discusses what happens when soil disappears. It also talks about different ways farmers can protect their fields from erosion. Imagine you need to convince a farmer to take steps to keep her fields from eroding. What method from this book would you recommend to the farmer? Write a short essay explaining your opinion. Make sure to give reasons for your opinion, as well as facts and details to support those reasons.

You Are There

This book discusses the Dust Bowl, a region of the United States where soil erosion created massive dust storms in the 1930s. Imagine you are living in that time, and there is a huge dust storm heading for your town. What do you see when you look outdoors? What are you worried about?

Say What?

Studying soil can mean learning a lot of new vocabulary. Find five words in this book you have never heard or read before. Use a dictionary to find their meanings. Then write the meanings in your own words, and use each word in a sentence.

GLOSSARY

desertification
the process by which fertile land becomes desert

drought
a long period of dry weather

erosion
the process of being carried away by the action of water, wind, or glacial ice

fungi
living beings, such as molds, mildews, and mushrooms, that live on dead or decaying organic matter

loam
a soil consisting of a loose, easily crumbled mixture of varying amounts of clay, silt, and sand

microbe
an organism of microscopic or less than microscopic size

mineral
a solid chemical element or compound that occurs naturally from nonliving matter

organic
obtained from living things

sediment
soil, stones, and sand deposited by water, wind, or glaciers

weathering
to change by exposure to the weather

LEARN MORE

Books

Bourgeois, Paulette, Kathy Vanderlinden, and Martha Newbigging. *The Dirt on Dirt*. Toronto: Kids Can, 2008.

Lay, Richard. *A Green Kid's Guide to Soil Preparation*. Minneapolis: ABDO, 2013.

Lindbo, David L., and Judy Mannes. *Soil! Get the Inside Scoop*. Madison, WI: Soil Science Society of America, 2008.

Websites

To learn more about Rocks and Minerals, visit **booklinks.abdopublishing.com**. These links are routinely monitored and updated to provide the most current information available.

Visit **www.mycorelibrary.com** for free additional tools for teachers and students.

INDEX

ABOUT THE AUTHOR

Rebecca E. Hirsch is a former scientist and the author of dozens of books on science and nature for young readers. She lives in Pennsylvania with her husband, three children, one cat, and a small flock of chickens.